# The Marriage Dictionary

*Double Eagle Press*

# The Marriage Dictionary

Written & Illustrated
by
Tom Carey

First published March, 1993.

Manufactured in the United States of America.

ISBN: 1-877590-99-1

Published by
*Double Eagle Press*
1124 N. Derbyshire
Arlington Hts., IL 60004

*For Kathy,*
*who said yes.*

# *A*

**Abstinence**   What your wife will want to practice during the three months prior to your wedding, even though you've been living together for two years, "Because it'll be so romantic on our wedding night."

**Alterations**   What your wife's gown will need the day before the wedding, when it is discovered that she has lost eighteen pounds and two dress sizes due to the month long pre-wedding diet of saltines and diet soda she went on so she'd "look good in my wedding photos."

**American Embassy**   Place you'll be spending your time on the little, out-of-the-way, undiscovered Caribbean island where your travel agent sends you on your honeymoon. (See *Coup*).

**Amnesia**  Odd medical condition which often afflicts husbands the day after a night out drinking and carousing with the boys.

**Anorexic**  The condition of the old girlfriends whose photos and love letters your husband still keeps in a shoe box on the top shelf of his closet. (See *Busty*).

**Argument**  Disagreement between you and your spouse, which will last the length of your marriage, interspersed with short periods of making up.

**Athlete**  What your husband still sees when he looks in the mirror.

**Athlete's Foot**  The only part of your husband that is still truly athletic.

# Amnesia

# B

**Baby**

1. Exclamation following exceptionally passionate sex. (*Ex.* "Baby, baby, baby!"). 2. Exclamation following positive home pregnancy test, nine months later. (*Ex.* "Baby, baby, baby?!").

**Bachelor**

Any single male friend, who has a discernable heartbeat and is between the ages of 20 and 80, who your wife will insist on trying to "set up" with her single friends and sisters.

**Bachelor Party**

All-male bash held the week before the wedding, in which the groom and all of his friends celebrate the many joys of being a single man by drinking until they vomit, gambling away their hard-earned money in card games, and

# Bachelor

by watching a nude woman with very large breasts bounce up and down to a boom box blasting the Rolling Stones. (See *Guilty*).

**Bachelorette Party**

All-female bash held the week before the wedding, in which the bride and all of her friends celebrate the many joys of being a single woman, by drinking until they pass out, talking behind the backs of all the women they know who aren't there, and by stuffing dollar bills into the G-string of a male erotic dancer who has the abdominal muscles of an Olympic gymnast. (See *Innocent*).

**Back Seat**

Where you will sit when your husband's mother is in the car. Also where wives will sit when "dating" another couple.

**Ballet**

Dance performed to classical music in an elegant theater before tearful, enraptured wives accompanied by bored, distracted husbands, who repeat, "He's gay, y'know" every time the lead male dancer receives applause from the audience.

**Bathrobe**

One of four Christmas gifts which you will be receiving from your husband every single year, now that you're married. (See *Nightgown, Perfume* and *Slippers*).

**Beer**

Carbonated, malt-based, alcohol beverage which, when drunk in quantity, will keep your husband chubby, out of shape, slow witted, gassy and sexually unappealling.

**Beer Commercial**

Television advertisement for carbonated, malt-based, alcohol beverage, shown at breaks in professional sporting events, which are meant to convince men that beer, when drunk in quantity, will make them slim, athletic, witty and sexually irresistible.

**Best Man**    Best friend of the groom, whose responsibilities at the wedding include: organizing the bachelor party, making sure the groom is not too hung over to get through a church wedding and repeatedly telling him, "It's still not too late to back out, you know..."

**Bikini**    1. Bathing suit which reveals every flaw and bit of flab, on your wife's body.    2. Small Pacific atoll thousands of miles from anyone, which is why it's the only place she'd ever consider wearing one.

**Bikini Line**    Area of wife's anatomy whose advance and retreat signify the passing of the seasons as accurately as the coat of the wooly caterpillar.

**Bimbo**    Any woman to whom you pay a compliment, while in the company of your wife. (*Ex.* You - "Bill's new wife is really attractive, isn't she?"  Your wife - "That bimbo?")

**Blue**   1. Color of the condom you receive as a gag gift at your shower. 2. Color of your face when said condom fails. 3. Color of the chemically treated swab in your Home Pregnancy Test Kit. 4. Color your husband will be painting the den,...I mean, nursery.

**Bouquet**   The flower arrangement carried by the bride who, during the bouquet tossing ceremony, will rifle it on a line to her best friend, who longs to become engaged to her long-time, cold-footed beau. (See *Garter*).

**Bowl Games**   Excuse for your husband to ignore you from December 1 through January 15 every year.

**Boy-Girl**   Seating arrangement of married couples which allows harmless, spouse-supervised flirting at dinner parties and theaters.

# Bowl Games

**Bra**   Decoration draped by your wife over the shower curtain rod in the bathroom. (See *Pantyhose*).

**Bridal Registry**   Service provided by department stores, which allows you and your spouse to keep track of exactly how much money your friends and relatives spending on gifts.

**Brides**   Magazine targeted to engaged women, which features six pages of articles on subjects like choosing a veil, or on the pros and cons of serving fruit cocktail at the reception, along with over 1200 pages of advertising for wedding gowns, china, glassware, tuxedo rentals, limosine services, caterers, disc jockeys and orchestras.

**Bridesmaids**   Friends and sisters of yours, for whom you have stood up over the years, spending thousands of dollars on shoes that don't fit, ridiculous hats, and dresses so

# Bridesmaid Dress

"Gone With The Wind"
Hat
$75

Shoulder
Pads
$7

Ugly
Necklace
and Earrings
$85

Push Up Bra
$30

Bustle
$10

Dress
$110

Gloves
$25

Petticoats
$15

Shoes
$60

Total $417.00

hideous looking that they have been collecting dust in the back of your closet ever since. Now, it's payback time.

**Bridesmaid Dress**

Frock worn by friends and sisters of yours, chosen by you to be so unflattering that even if you wake up on your wedding day looking eerily like a cathedral gnome, you will appear gorgeous in comparison to them.

**Busty**

The condition of the old girlfriends whose photos and love letters your husband keeps in a shoe box on the top shelf of his closet. (See *Anorexic*).

# C

**Car**

Where you'll spend most of the holiday season, now that you have a dozen in-laws to visit.

**Cat**

Animal you would like as a pet but that your husband *claims* to be allergic to. (See *Dog*).

**Celibate**

What the priest who gives you your church-required pre-marital sexual counseling is.

**Chair**

Something your husband used to hold for you.

**Cheap**

What your spouse is, when it comes to spending his or her own money. (See *Frugal*).

**China**

1. The expensive plates, bowls, saucers, cups and dishes that you will be receiving from various friends, relatives and guests at your wedding. 2. Where 1 billion people who don't give a damn about your wedding live.

**Chores**

Day to day household tasks which you and your spouse pledge to divide equally, but will end up being done by whoever gets fed up with filth the quickest.

**Closet**

1. Storage areas in your new home which will be divided on an as needed basis: 93% for you, 7% to your husband. 2. What your cousin Blaine from San Francisco will come out of, in front of 250 startled guests at your wedding reception, after drinking a couple of bottles of champagne.

**Coat**

Something your husband used to hold for you.

# Cold

**Cocooning**    What your husband calls staying at home every evening, sprawled out on the couch in his sweat clothes, drinking beer and zapping through cable TV channels with the remote.

**Cold**    1. Illness characterized by the following symptoms in husbands: coughing, sneezing, sore throat, runny nose, whining, need for constant attention, desire for tea and toast with strawberry preserves spread on just the way Mom used to, three full days off of work and ten full days off of chores because "I have a cold, you know, it could turn into pnuemonia."    2. Relative sexual temperature of wife after waiting on sick, whiny husband for two weeks.

**Cologne**    One of four Christmas gifts which you will be receiving from your wife every single year, now that you're married.  (See *Gloves*, *Scarf*, and *Tie*).

**Commitment**  What your fiance was able to make to his job, his poker game, his tee time, his mother and his favorite fishing TV show, more easily than he was to you.

**Conversing**  What you are doing when you talk about your neighbors' marital difficulties. (See *Gossiping*).

**Cotton**  Material from which a married woman's underwear is made. (See *Silk*).

**Coup**  Military take-over which will occur on the little, out-of-the-way, undiscovered Caribbean island where your travel agent sends you on your honeymoon. (See *American Embassy*).

**Cuddle**  Act of warmth and affection that your husband will inevitably interpret as foreplay. (See *Kiss*, *Hug*, and *Snuggle*).

# Cuddle

# D

**D.J.**   Entertainer hired to play music at your wedding reception, who will disregard all requests for *your* favorite songs, and instead get drunk as a skunk and play, "Celebration", the version of "Mony Mony" with the dirty lyrics and "Shout", during which he will holler, "Every-body do the Gator!" and then throw himself on the floor in an attempt to look under the bridesmaid's dresses.

**Dance**   The action of moving rhythmically to music with a partner, a skill which a woman posesses naturally, but which a man acquires only for the short time in his young adulthood when he wishes to meet and impress young women, and abandons thereafter due to mysterious "knee injuries".

**Date**    Social engagement between two people who are still trying to decide whether or not it would be safe to sleep together.

**Dog**    Animal you would like as a pet, but that your wife *claims* to be allergic to. (See *Cat*).

**Door**    Something your husband used to hold for you.

**Doubles**    1. Tennis game played by athletic couples who wish to burn a few calories while arguing. 2. Size of drinks they order afterward.

**Driveway**    Where your husband will sit, in his idling automobile, honking the horn and yelling, while you try to get ready to go out.

**Duck**    1. Design motif on all your wife's plates, cups, saucers, bowls, dishes

# Doubles

and various ceramic knick-knacks. 2. What you'll need to do when you make fun of one of your wife's plates, cups, saucers, bowls, dishes, and various ceramic knick-knacks.

**Dysfunctional**  State of your relationship according to your wife who up and screams at you like a madwoman every couple of weeks, for no apparent reason, when all you're trying to do is watch a little TV. (See *Relationship*).

# E

**Early**
1. What your husband insists on being, everywhere you go together ("The invitation *says* 7:00!")
2. What he is in bed, too.

**Elope**
1. What your parents secretly wish that you would do, after they volunteer to "help" with the wedding. 2. What you seriously consider doing after a couple of months of your parents' "help".

**Emerge**
What your left breast will do, from the top of your strapless gown, during a spirited rendition of the "Chicken Dance."

**Encore**
What your wife will want after sex on your wedding night. (See *ZZZ's*).

# Elope

**Engagement**  A period of time which two people who have decided to get married take, in order to provide plenty of time for their in-laws to argue about seating arrangements for the reception, for the caterers to go out of business, for several bridesmaids to dye their shoes the wrong color and for the minister to quit the clergy and run off to Acapulco with the church organist. Who has the wedding music.

**Engraving**  Expensive printing process, that you will use on your wedding invitations, napkins and matchbooks, all of which will have your spouse's name spelled wrong.

**Erotica**  Any sexually explicit material that your wife enjoys, but that you find boring. (See *Pornography*).

**ESP**  An abbreviation for extrasensory perception, an ability your wife will expect you to possess.

# ESP

**Ex**

1. Your wife's previous husband, who she will remember as a scummy, rotten, two-timing, low-down loser, before your marriage. 2. Your wife's previous husband, who she will remember as a loving, tender, romantic example of everything you are not, after your marriage.

**Exchanging**

What your rich aunt and uncle will catch you doing with the very expensive, but not very tasteful, wedding gift they gave you.

# F

**Fat**  The chance that you will still be allowed to play in your weekly poker game after you're married.

**Feelings**  1. Song that the band at your wedding reception will play three times in two hours.  2. What your husband will discuss three times in two years.

**Forehead**  One of your husband's two body parts which will grow larger after marriage. (See *Stomach*).

**Foreplay**  1. (First year of marriage) A prelude to intercourse, which lasts up to an hour or more and includes kissing, stroking, cuddling, fondling, back rubs, hot oil massages, candlelit dinners, drives along the beach, tender declarations of love and slow dancing to Tony Bennett records. 2. (After first year of marriage) A pinch on the ass.

**Frederick's Of Hollywood**  Store where your wife bought her underwear before you were married. (See *J.C. Penney's*).

**Freeloader**  Any friend of your spouse who visits and sleeps on your couch, eats all your food, leaves little hairs in your bath soap and ends up staying twice as long you expect him to. (See *Guest*).

**Frugal**  What *you* are, when it comes to spending your own money. (See *Cheap*).

**Fuller**  The cut of the Levi's that you'll have to buy for your husband, so he can claim, "I still wear the same size jeans I wore in high school."

# Fuller

# G

**Garage Sale**  Event held to sell all the items you bought with your spouse's money (at about 25 cents on the dollar) after your spouse finds out about it and files for divorce. (See *Joint Bank Account*).

**Garter**  Bit of lingerie you are supposed to remove from your wife's leg during the reception and toss, per her instructions, to her best friend's long-time cold-footed beau. Her plans will be dashed when said beau is in the bathroom during the ceremony, allowing the garter to be snagged by your annoying 12-year-old nephew, who will pester the bride's best friend for the rest of the night saying, "Hey, baby, when's the honeymoon?"

**Garter Belt**     1. Item of lingerie you use to keep your stockings up. 2. Item of lingerie you use to keep your husband's penis up.

**Gene**     1. The part of the human chromosome which insures that you and your spouse will eventually look, sound, behave and deteriorate just like your parents. 2. The part of the human chromosome which insures that your children will eventually look, sound, behave and deteriorate just like you.

**Gifts**     Cash and presents whose value reflects how much you are liked by your friends and relatives and how much *you* spent on *them* when *they* got married.

**Gloves**     One of four Christmas gifts which you will be receiving from your wife every single year, now that you're married. (See *Cologne, Scarf* and *Tie*).

# Gifts

**Gossiping**   What the neighbors are doing when they talk about you and your spouse's marital difficulties. (See *Conversing*).

**Gray**   The color of your husband's Jockey shorts. (See *Pink* and *White*).

**Greeting Card**   Small token of your love and affection for your wife, featuring a syrupy verse and a drawing of a young couple holding hands and making goo-goo eyes at one another, which you will be sending to her at frequent intervals throughout your relationship, "just because I was thinking of you, Honey." If you know what's good for you.

**Grocery List**   Lengthy, detailed list of food items and household products that your husband will leave on the kitchen table when he goes to the store, returning instead with six cartons of Nestles' Crunch Ice Cream Bars, a head of lettuce, a tomato (because he knows how much you like salad), a *Car & Driver* Magazine, a loaf of Wonder bread, a jar of peanut butter, a jar of grape jelly and a box of day-old (30% off!) chocolate doughnuts.

**Groom**　　Least important member of wedding party, whose only duties are to show up on time, remember the ring and try not to be drunk.

**Guest**　　Any friend of *yours* who visits and sleeps on your couch, eats all your food, leaves little hairs in your bath soap and ends up staying twice as long you expect him to. (See *Freeloader*).

**Guilty**　　The way your husband will act when you question him about what went on at his bachelor party.

# H

**Hair**　What will begin disappearing from your husband's head and appearing in his nose and ears, soon after you exchange vows.

**Hairy**　1. Husband's razor after you use it. 2. The fight that occurs after your husband tries to use his razor after you do and loses a quart of blood down the bathroom sink.

**Hand**　Something your husband used to hold for you.

**Here Comes The Bride**　1. Song that is played by church organist as you walk down the aisle after the wedding ceremony. 2. Phrase that your husband will utter jokingly during a crucial moment of wedding night love-making, which will cause you to lose your concentration. And temper.

**Home**          What a house is called during marriage. (See *Real Estate*)

**Home Pregnancy Test**      Small, chemically treated strip that your husband will frantically run to the drugstore to purchase each time your period is more than 12 hours late.

**Honey**          Term of endearment used by newlyweds meaning "bee vomit."

**Honeymoon**     Trip newlyweds take to exotic, romantic resort to discover passion, love and what their spouse really does in the bathroom.

**House**         Domicile purchased by married couples so they have someplace to pour all their money.

# Hyphen

**Hug**

Act of warmth and affection that your husband will inevitably interpret as foreplay. (See *Kiss*, *Cuddle* and *Snuggle*).

**Hunting**

Male Bonding Ritual which your husband and several of his pals use as an excuse to drive four-wheel-drive vehicles, fire large, powerful weapons, go to the bathroom out of doors and mercilessly slaughter God's warm, fuzzy little creatures.

**Hyphen**

Punctuation mark added to the end of a modern wife's last name along with the name of her new husband. Truly enlightened husbands will also add a hyphen and their wife's last name. Which leads to names like Richard and Mary Kreitzer-Abramowitz. Which leads to children with serious identity, not to mention spelling, problems.

# I

**Ice Pack**   Plastic pouch filled with ice commonly used to reduce swelling in head injuries. (See *Idiot*).

**Idiot**   Word you use to describe your new 6' 4", 230 lb., brother-in-law at your wedding, unaware that he is right behind you. (See *Ice Pack*).

**"I'll Let You Know"**   No.

**Imaginative**   Any idea *you* come up with to enliven sex which your spouse finds too gross. (See *Kinky*).

**Impotence**   Physical manifestation of a husband's lack of sexual desire due most often to stress, to alcohol

# Imaginative

consumption or to his wife's in-sistence on wearing flannel night-gowns and face cream to bed.

**Inch**   Unit of measure whose length is consistently underestimated by men.

**Incontinence**   Condition which your spouse's great aunt Sylvia suffers from, as many of the guests at your wed-ding reception will discover when she is seated at the table farthest from the ladies room.

**Ingrown**   What your wife's toenails will be after ten hours of having her feet crammed into shoes that are two sizes too small but which she bought anyway because they were the only ones she really liked with her dress.

**In-Law**   Person from your spouse's side of the family who you never met

# In-Law

before, but who will show up the week before your wedding, sleep on your living room couch, spend hours in your bathroom and eat up all your Oreo's. This person will give you a wedding gift of ceramic "Welcome to Wisconsin" salt and pepper shakers in the shape of cows.

**Innocent**    The way your wife will act when you question her about what went on at her bachelorette party.

**Insomnia**    Condition your husband will insist you must be suffering from when you complain that you can't sleep due to his endless snoring, thrashing, talking and tooth-grinding.

**Intestinal**    The kind of virus about a third of your guests will develop after enjoying the lovely seafood buffet at your wedding reception.

**Invitations**     The cards you sent to request the presence, and presents, of 350 of your closest friends, relatives and co-workers at your wedding reception. Your fiancee will find forty of them, the ones that you gave him to mail six weeks before your wedding day, in the inside pocket of his coat, three days before your wedding day.

**Involuntary**     The charge you can probably
**Manslaughter**     plead to after you kill him.

# J

**J.C. Penney's**
Store where your wife buys her underwear since you got married. (See *Frederick's of Hollywood*).

**Jabba The Hut**
Movie character on whose remarkable resemblence to your new mother-in-law you comment, after several cocktails at the rehearsal dinner, nearly causing your wedding to be called off.

**Jack**
Indispensible tire changing tool, the lack of which will leave you and most of your wedding party stranded on the median of the expressway, when the limo blows a tire on the way from the church to the reception.

# Jewelry Appraiser

**Jello**     The only food your husband has ever learned to "cook".

**Jelly Jar**     Glass container with pictures of Yogi Bear and Boo Boo on the side, which your husband will insist on using as a drinking glass, despite the hundreds of dollars worth of elegant glassware you got as wedding gifts.

**Jewelry Appraiser**     Professional gemstone expert to whom your fiancee will take her engagement ring only hours after you give it to her. This will enable her to insure it for its proper value so it will be safe, and to see if you spent at least two month's salary, so you will be.
(See *Two Month's Salary*).

**Joint Bank Account**     Checking account which allows you to spend your spouse's money any way that you want.
(See *Garage Sale*).

# K

**Kayak**    Notoriously unstable boat that your spouse will insist on renting during your honeymoon, even though he knows you can't swim. (See *Saltwater*).

**Kids**    Result of spontaneous, exciting, passionate sex whose arrival will prevent you from having spontaneous, exciting, passionate sex ever again.

**Kilt**    What your Scottish father-in-law will wear to your wedding. (See *Nothing*).

**Kinky**    Any idea your spouse comes up with to enliven sex, which you think is gross. (See *Imaginative*).

# Kayak

**Kiss**  Act of warmth and affection that your husband will inevitably interpret as foreplay. (See *Hug, Cuddle* and *Snuggle*).

**Kitchen**  Place in your home where everyone will gather during your post-wedding, pre-reception party, even though you spent three days cleaning every room in the house but that one.

**Kleenex**  The one item you will forget to take with you down the aisle which will result in your making a loud, wet, snuffling sound every ten seconds during the ceremony. "I (sniffle) Janine Marie Cosgrove (snort) take this man (slurf) to be my lawfully (snark) wedded (sniff) husband..."

# Kleenex

# L

**Labor**  What your eight-and-a-half-months-pregnant sister, and Maid of Honor, will go into during your wedding vows.

**Last Name**  What your husband will want you to change, even though you have built a successful career and business with it and even though yours is Johnson and his is Wizenjoskowicz.

**Late**  1. What your wife will inevitably be when you're in a hurry to get to a party. 2. What her period will be a couple of weeks after that party where you both had a few too many drinks, forgot to go to the drugstore, and figured "Oh, what the hell. One time won't make any difference."

# Late

**Limerick**  Risque, five line poem your new father-in-law will recite for your tremendously straitlaced mother. (See *Nantucket*).

**Lingerie**  Ill-fitting, unflattering and often downright strange looking underwear that you will receive from your husband as a birthday gift after he watches *9 1/2 Weeks* for the first time.

**Lip Waxing**  Procedure used to remove hair from upper lip that will tear a hunk of skin out of your face two days before your wedding.

**Lukewarm**  1. Temperature of the champagne served at your wedding reception. 2. The reaction of your in-laws to the news that you'll be moving in with them for awhile, "Just 'til we get on our feet."

# Limerick

# M

**Maid Of Honor**

Bride's closest friend, who the groom will meet for the first time at the rehearsal dinner, and either fall madly in love with, thereby delaying the wedding plans, or hate intensely, thereby delaying the wedding plans.

**Male Bonding Ritual**

Handy excuse for your husband to engage in infantile behavior with his buddies. Including, but not limited to, bowling, softball, poker, any spectator sport where there is a chance of severe injury to the participants, and any activity that includes beer drinking.

**Map**

Chart which your husband is unable to read and which you are unable to fold.

# Maid Of Honor

**Marriage**     Sacred relationship between a man and a woman, in which they promise to love, honor and cherish one another, even after their body parts begin to wrinkle, sag and cease to function properly.

**Marriage Counselor**     Professional who will help you and your spouse to communicate more efficiently, to discuss disagreements in a fair and rational manner and to divide the responsibilities of your marriage so that you will be able to celebrate your love for one another, enjoy your marriage and stay together long enough for her to make a down payment on a new BMW.

**Maybe**     No.

**Metabolism**     The human body's ability to burn calories, which slows down drastically as you get older, which must be the reason you and your spouse are no longer able to fit comforta-

bly in theater seats, and not because you let your joint health
club membership lapse and have
taken to breakfasting on Hostess
Twinkies and Coca-Cola.

**Minister**  Clergyman who will perform
your wedding ceremony, even
though you and your spouse ha-
ven't been to church in years,
have lived together out-of-
wedlock and are only doing the
"church thing" for the relatives.
He will be unable to resist drawl-
ing a few obvious sarcastic com-
ments about the decline in the na-
tion's moral fiber during his ser-
mon.

**Mold**  1. What you will desperately try to
do to your husband's manners,
hygenic practices and housekeep-
ing habits. 2. What will grow on
your husband's shower curtain
when you fail in your attempt and
move out.

**Money**    Something that married couples rarely have, but seem to be able to argue about anyway.

**Monsoon**    The season it will be on the little, out-of-the-way, undiscovered Caribbean island where your travel agent sends you on your honeymoon.

**Mother**    Your female parent who is an expert on homemaking, cooking, childcare, entertaining, home buying, health, fashion and travel.

**Mother-In-Law**    Your spouse's female parent who *thinks* she's an expert on homemaking, cooking, childcare, entertaining, home buying, health, fashion and travel.

# Monsoon

# N

**Nantucket**     Town on Cape Cod in Massachusetts where the man in your father-in-law's favorite limerick is from. (See *Limerick*).

**Nap**     What your grandfather, who has a deviated septum and consequently snores like a freight train, will take in the front pew, during your wedding ceremony.

**Neighbors**     People who live near you, who are never around when you need to borrow power tools or jumper cables, but who are everywhere when you are having a heated argument with your spouse.

**Nest Egg**     The money that you were saving for your retirement, that your

# Nest Egg

husband will invest with a friend of a friend who knows a guy whose cousin has a "can't-miss" stock tip. (See *Zip*).

**Newlywed**   What you and your spouse will officially be considered until your first anniversary, or until you go an entire week without sex, whichever comes first.

**Nightgown**   One of four Christmas gifts which you will be receiving from your husband every single year, now that you're married. (See *Bathrobe*, *Perfume* and *Slippers*).

**No Shows**   What twelve people who sent in their RSVP's for your reception will be, costing you $650 in un-eaten fruit cocktail, soup, salad, chicken Kiev and sherbet.

**Nothing**   What he will be wearing underneath it. (See *Kilt*).

# Nothing

**Notre Dame**     University in South Bend, Indiana, whose football team will be playing the afternoon of your wedding day, which is why all the men in the wedding party will be gathered around a TV in the bar next door during your entire reception.

**Numb**     What your face will be after six straight hours of smiling for wedding pictures.

# O

**Obey**   The word in the traditional wedding vows which follows "to love, honor and...".  Upon hearing this word your wife will snort loudly and say, "When pigs fly, buster," loudly enough for the minister, guests, video cameraman and many of the shoppers at the mall next door to hear.

**Oboe**   1. One of the most beautiful sounding, but difficult to play, classical woodwind instruments. 2. Instrument which your wife's Aunt Betty will insist her young son Otto play at your wedding.

**Ode To Joy**   1. One of the most beautiful sounding, but difficult to play, classical music pieces. 2. Piece young Otto will choose to "play".

**Off White**  The color of the dress your mother-in-law suggests you *ought* to be wearing at your wedding.

**Oh**  What your husband says, when you say, "I love you," to him, while he's watching a playoff game on TV.

**Oh Oh**  What your husband says, during the commercial break, when he gets up to go to the bathroom and finds that you have stuffed all his favorite ties down the toilet.

**Okra**  The only vegetable your caterer will be able to find, after a power outage knocks out his refrigerators, spoiling 90% of the food you had originally planned to serve at your reception.

**Optical Illusion**  What your wife will insist it was that you saw at the reception, when you could have sworn she

# Oh Oh

was kissing the very handsome lead singer of the band passionately on the lips.

**Orange**     The tint of your skin after you burn, then peel, then use that phony tan make-up that you bought in the drugstore on your way home from the airport, after your honeymoon on the little, out-of-the-way, undiscovered Caribbean island where your travel agent sends you during monsoon season.

**Orphan**     What you'll wish you had been when you see the outfit your mother has planned to wear to your wedding.

**Orthodontia**     What you'll need to begin saving for now, if you plan to have kids.

# P

**PMS**     Malady which afflicts your wife during the twenty-five days of the month when she's not having her period.

**Pantyhose**     Decoration hung by wives over the shower curtain rod in the bathroom. (see *Bra*).

**Paper**     What most of your meals come wrapped in, now that you're married and you both work.

**Penis**     Part of male anatomy which contains the brain.

**Perfume**     One of four Christmas gifts which you will be receiving from your husband every single year, now that you're married. (See *Bathrobe*, *Nightgown* and *Slippers*).

**Perhaps**     No.

**Period**     The five days of the month when your wife does not have PMS.

**Personality Disorders**     Any of the enormously destructive habits (like fingernail chewing, door slamming and drinking milk straight out of the carton) that your spouse has, any of which could indicate a need for psychiatric help. (See *Quirk*).

**Pink**     Color of your husband's Jockey shorts after he washes them with your red sweatshirt. (See *Gray* and *White*).

**Pizza**     What husband means when he says "My night to cook."

# Pizza

**Poker**

1. Card game played once a month by your husband, during which he and his stupid friends drink too much, gamble too much, smoke fat, smelly cigars and stay out until all hours. 2. Kind of face put on by your husband when he says that he "didn't drink too much, lose too much or stay out too late." 3. Fireplace implement you swing at your husband after he tells you all those lies.

**Prenuptial Agreement**

Legal document signed by a husband and wife, in which they agree on the distribution of assets in the event of divorce, but which neglects to cover really important marital issues, like who gets to use the bathroom first in the morning.

# Prenuptial Agreement

**Quack**
The doctor who told your eight-weeks-pregnant wife that her abdominal discomfort and nausea was "Just a little heartburn."

**Quaint**
Description in the brochure of the drafty, roach-infested, bed & breakfast, where you and your wife spend a long awaited get-away weekend with the owner Ray Bob, his lovely wife (and cousin) Jimmie Sue, their ten kids and various barnyard animals.

**Quality**
The kind of sex your wife wants. (See *Quantity*).

**Quantity**
The kind of sex your husband wants. (See *Quality*).

**Quirk**     Any of the totally harmless little
              habits you have (like fingernail
              chewing, door slamming and
              drinking milk straight from the
              carton) that drive your spouse
              crazy. (See *Personality Disorder*).


**Quiver**    1. What your wife used to do in
              lustful anticipation of whatever
              new and exciting sexual game you
              came up with. 2. What your wife
              does now in revulsion at the
              thought of whatever new and ex-
              citing sexual game you're going to
              come up with next.

# R

**RSVP Cards**  Cards sent out with a wedding invitation, which may be returned to the bride at any time, even in the vestibule before the ceremony, which indicate a desire to attend the wedding reception and which may be amended to include extra guests, children and pets.

**Real Estate**  What your house is called during divorce proceedings. (See *Home*)

**Rehearsal**  Get together held the night before the wedding during which the bride and groom learn where they'll stand at church during the wedding ceremony.

**Rehearsal Dinner**  Get together held the night before the wedding during which the

# RSVP Cards

bride and groom learn where they'll stand with their in-laws after the wedding ceremony.

**Relationship**  Personal arrangement between you and your husband, wherein *he* agrees to sit like a lump on the couch, silently zapping from channel to channel searching for some TV show which has apparently yet to be developed because he never stops at one long enough to see what program is on, unless there is a naked woman on, in which case he turns the sound way down so as to fool you into thinking that he's not watching soft porn, and wherein *you* agree to do all the chores, remember all his families' birthdays and scream at him about every three weeks that he's driving you crazy. (See *Dysfunctional*).

**Religion**  Organization of people with a set of deeply-held, sacred and traditional spiritual beliefs which you will have to adopt for a few weeks if you want to have your wedding at a really cool church.

**Remote**  1. The only household appliance, besides the refrigerator, that your husband is capable of operating properly.  2. The chance that you will get to see more than two minutes of any TV show, if he has control of it.

**Restaurant**  Public eating establishment which will be at its most crowded the night you present your girlfriend with a "surprise" diamond engagement ring, which she will then turn down, loudly and firmly, before walking out in front of the maitre'd, the strolling violinist, the waitress, the girl who sells roses, the busboy and dozens of your fellow diners.

**Reunion**  Get together of former high school classmates, which your

# Romance

spouse will want to attend alone, in order to spare you the boredom of listening to all that reminiscing and in order to try to get something going with an old flame.

**Rightside Up**    They way you (and your mother, and her mother) put glasses in the cupboard. (See *Upside Down*).

**Ring**    1. Finger ornament couples bestow upon one another that symbolizes eternity. 2. High water mark on bathtub which symbolizes that husband hasn't cleaned it in eternity.

**Romance**    What will go out of your marriage when your wife comes into the bathroom while you're brushing your teeth and plops down on the toilet.

# S

**Saltwater**     What you will barf up on the beach after your spouse tips your kayak over, drags you to the beach and administers CPR. (See *Kayak*).

**Scarf**     One of four Christmas gifts which you will be receiving from your wife every single year, now that you're married. (See *Cologne*, *Gloves* and *Tie*).

**Seating Arrangement**     Layout of dining area at your reception which, no matter how often you reorganize it, will end up having your husband's Uncle Ralph, with the drinking problem, next to the bar, your cousin Susan at the same table with your husband's brother Ed, who she used to date and now hates, and his new wife with the huge

# Scarf

breasts, and your least favorite aunt and uncle at the same table with his least favorite aunt and uncle, who will all turn out to like each other so much that they'll plan a return trip to visit you next month and stay at "your place because it's so nice and you've got so dang much room."

**Sex**     What couples do in bed before marriage. (See *Sleep*).

**Silk**     Material from which a single woman's underwear is made. (See *Cotton*).

**Sink**     What your hopes will do, when you wake up one day to find yourself staring across the breakfast table at the sleepy face of your spouse, and you realize that you will be waking up to that face each morning for the rest of your life. 2. Place in your bathroom where your husband collects whiskers.

**Sleep**  What couples do in bed after marriage. (See *Sex*).

**Slippers**  One of four Christmas gifts which you will be receiving from your husband every single year, now that you're married. (See *Bathrobe*, *Nightgown* and *Perfume*).

**Snuggle**  Act of warmth and affection that your husband will inevitably interpret as foreplay. (See *Kiss*, *Cuddle* and *Hug*).

**Soap**  1. Bar or liquid placed on edge of sink by husbands, for washing hands. 2. Tiny heart-shaped and perfumed items placed in crystal dish on edge of sink by wife, not to be used for washing hands. (See *Towels*).

**Soap Opera**  1. Television dramas that your wife watches constantly, which feature lots of sex, lying, decep-

tion, divorce, lawsuits, crime and all-around despicable behavior.
2. Your in-laws' personal dramas, details of which your wife listens to constantly, which feature lots of sex, lying, deception, divorce, lawsuits, crime and all-around despicable behavior.

**Someday**     Never.

**Soon**     Later.

**Spoon**     Item of expensive flatware you'll receive as a gift, which your husband will use to stir paint when he can't find anything else.

**Stomach**     One of your husband's two body parts which will grow larger after marriage. (See *Forehead*).

**Stripper**     Chubby, fortyish, stretch-marked "professional entertainer" who

# Soap

will "perform" at your bachelor party by twirling around in circles and removing her clothing. She will also end up performing at your brother's bachelor party, your best friend's bachelor party, your best friend's brother's thirtieth birthday party, and your bosses' retirement bash. Soon you will be on a first name basis with her and may even begin exchanging Christmas cards.

**Stud**

1. Piece of lumber used to brace wallboard in home construction, which your husband will buy in large quantity in order to "finish" your basement. 2. What using power tools, get sawdust all over himself and wearing that manly leather tool belt make him feel like. Which is the only real reason he bought all that lumber in the first place.

**Surprise**

The kind of party your wife will throw for you at every milestone

# Stud

birthday, even though you have begged her repeatedly not to. It will include insufferable coworkers bearing gag gifts, relatives and in-laws who you can't stand, nosy neighbors who are there mostly for the free food and all your married couple friends, who will now expect you to help plan and execute *their* surprise parties.

**Sweat Pants**     One of the items your wife will begin wearing to bed after you're married. (See *Wool Socks* and *X-Large T-Shirt*).

# Surprise

# T

**Tan**
What you will try to get in the only two sunny days of your honeymoon. (See *Third Degree*).

**Television**
An electronic marital aid which will keep you from being bored if you leave it on during sex.

**Testosterone**
Hormone which causes facial hair, muscularity, a deep voice, speeding tickets, the desire to watch professional wrestling *and* Arnold Shwarzenegger movies, war, fist fights, and the need to purchase cocktails for women with names like "Boom Boom".

**Third Degree**
The kind of burn you will get on your honeymoon. (See *Tan*).

# Television

**Tie**
One of four Christmas gifts which you will be receiving from your wife every single year, now that you're married. (See *Cologne*, *Gloves* and *Scarf*).

**Tiff**
Any oral disagreement between you and your spouse which does not result in a visit from the police or a trip to the emergency room for stitches.

**Toast**
Touching and emotional moment during the wedding reception when the best man will take the microphone, ask for everyone's attention, and tell a rambling story about all the women in the groom's past who couldn't quite manage to get him to the altar. This will include their names, current whereabouts and a detailed physical description of each one, and will be captured on videotape so you can enjoy it for years to come.

# Toast

**Toilet Seat**　　Part of toilet which, despite the laws of physics, develops the ability to defy gravity immediately after you begin sharing your bathroom with your husband.

**Toilet Seat Cover**　　Fuzzy item your wife will place over the toilet seat lid, which is warm, cozy, color coordinated with the towels and wallpaper, and which will make it impossible for you to pee without holding it up with one hand.

**Towels**　　1. Terrycloth items hung near sink by husband for drying hands.
2. Small, lacy, decorative cloths hung near sink by wife for *not* drying hands.
(See *Soap*).

**Trash**　　The only thing in the house that your husband takes out less often than you.

**Trivia**  Any subject your spouse brings up during your favorite TV show.

**Tub**  What you turn into after you get married and no longer feel the need to watch your weight.

**Turkey**  1. Traditional Thanksgiving meal you always have to eat with your spouse's Uncle Ed.
2. Your spouse's Uncle Ed.

**Tuxedo**  Formal attire for men, designed so that even the most fashion-sense-deprived among them can look good for at least the hour or two it takes to get through the ceremony and picture taking.

**Two Month's Salary**  Figure designated by jewelry retailers as the amount you must spend on that tiny bit of metal and rock that you give your fiancee so she won't think you're cheap.
(See *Jewelry Appraiser*).

# U

**Umbrella**     Portable rain shelter which is available on the little, out-of-the-way, undiscovered Caribbean island where your travel agent sends you on your honeymoon during monsoon season, on the black market for $250.

**Uncapped**     The way your spouse always leaves the toothpaste tube, which lets the toothpaste harden into a shiny crust around the top, until the morning you squeeze the tube so hard in an effort to dispense a usable amount that it bursts free all at once, with enough force to send you crashing into the tub.

**Underarm**     Area of your body which, on your wedding day, will perspire at a rate that will keep your gown sat-

# Uncapped

urated, despite deodorant, talcum powder and dress shields.

**Underexposed**  The condition of every single roll of film shot at your wedding.

**Unpack**  What the customs inspector on the little, out-of-the-way, undiscovered Caribbean island where your travel agent sends you on your honeymoon will make you do, even though you're late for your flight, even though there's not another one until tomorrow and even though there are thirty other people in line who look like extras from a Miami Vice rerun.

**Upside Down**  The way your spouse puts glasses in the cupboard.
(See *Rightside Up*).

**Usher**  Job given to any male friends who you don't like quite enough to be a groomsmen.

# V

**Vacuum**

1. Electrical household appliance whose operation will remain a complete mystery to your husband even though he is able to disassemble and reassemble an automobile engine blindfolded. 2. State of your husband's brain during football season.

**Victoria's Secret**

Catalog your husband reads in the bathroom since you made him cancel his subscription to Playboy.

**Videotape**

1. What your husband will want to make while you're having sex during honeymoon. 2. What your husband will want to rent, instead of having sex, six months later.

**Virgin**

1. U.S. governed islands in the Carribbean Sea, where couples who aren't clients of *your* travel agent frequently honeymoon.
2. What your wife will want to act like on your honeymoon night, even if she's had more pairs of shoes under her bed than Howard Johnson's.

**Vote**

What you and your spouse cast each election year, even though you know that you disagree right down the line politically, and that you will cancel one another out.

**Vow**

1. Promise you make while kneeling before the altar on your wedding day, to love, honor and cherish your spouse for the rest of your life. 2. Promise you make while kneeling before the toilet on your wedding night to never drink two quarts of warm champagne, five glasses of wine and twelve beers in one night again for the rest of your life.

# Virgin

# W

**Wallpaper**  Decorative wall covering in your home or apartment, which was acceptable to your wife during the three years you lived together, but which she can not bear to look at, now that you're married.

**We'll See**  No.

**White**  Color most of your husband's Jockey shorts must have been at one time. (See *Gray* and *Pink*).

**Whoopee Cushion**  Novelty gag gift of the type you will be receiving from your husband on your birthday now that you're married and he no longer feels romantic gifts are necessary.

**Wool Socks**    One of the items your wife will begin wearing to bed after you're married. (See *Sweat Pants* and *X-Large T-Shirt*).

**X Chromosome**

Sex chromosome responsible for, among other things, the desire for dust ruffles, pillow shams, pot pourris, soap operas and ballroom dancing.

**X-Large T-Shirt**

One of the items your wife will begin wearing to bed after you're married. (See *Sweat Pants* and *Wool Socks*).

**Xerox**

1. Machine at your husband's office on which, under the influence of several beers, he will sit with his pants down, in order to make grainy, black and white, but very identifiable photocopies of his butt. 2. Machine at your local print shop on which your husband will make several hundred photocopies of his resume.

# Xerox

# Y

**Y Chromosome**
Chromosome responsible for, among other things, the desire to pee out of doors, yell "Free Bird" at classical piano recitals, wear baseball caps backwards, chew tobacco and spit.

**Yam**
Variety of sweet potato, popular at Thanksgiving, that you are never able to prepare quite the same way your husband's mother does.

**Yawn**
1. The involuntary intake of air with wide open mouth, due to boredom or fatigue. 2. What you will be doing when the video photographer has your face in a tight close-up, during the part of your wedding ceremony where your wife tearfully reads to you the vows she wrote herself.

**Year**   The exact length of time that will pass from the day you get married to the day you forget your first anniversary.

**Yell**   What your spouse will accuse you of doing during an argument, even though you are just speaking loudly and clearly in an effort to get a point across to the INSUFFERABLY SMUG, BRAIN-DEAD IDIOT!

**Yes**   Maybe.

**YMCA**   Club you'll join on the "family plan" in a burst of New Year's resolution fitness energy and visit a total of six times in twelve months.

**Your Breath**   What you needn't bother holding, while waiting for your husband to hold the door, your chair, your coat or your hand anymore.

# Yell

# Z

**Zip**    What will be left of your nest egg after your husband invests it with a friend of a friend who knows a guy who has a cousin with a "can't-miss" stock tip.
(See *Nest Egg*).

**ZZZ's**    What your husband will want after sex on your wedding night.
(See *Encore*).

About the author:
Tom Carey
is a writer/illustrator/singer/songwriter
from Chicago, who has never had,
as yet, an actual job.